Graphic Organizers in Science™

Learning About Weather with Graphic Organizers

Diana Estigarribia

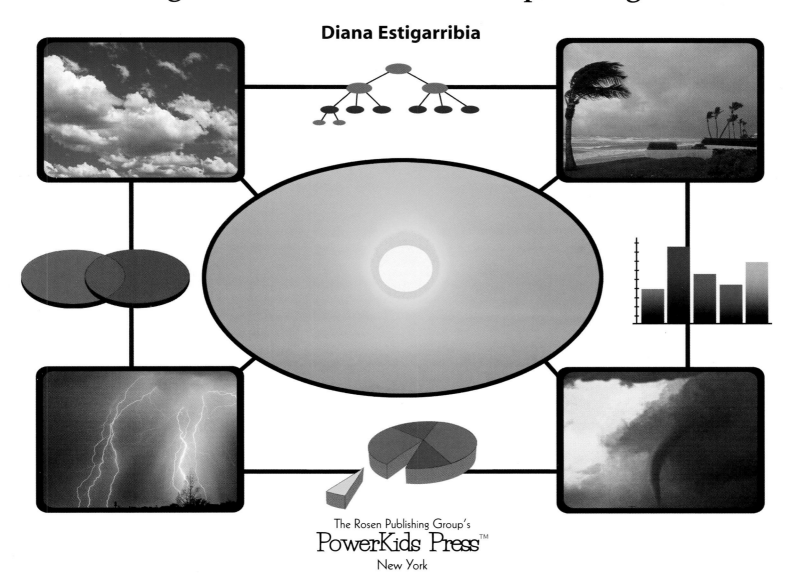

The Rosen Publishing Group's
PowerKids Press™
New York

For my parents, Concepción and Augusto, with love

Published in 2005 by The Rosen Publishing Group, Inc.
29 East 21st Street, New York, NY 10010

First Edition

Editor: Natashya Wilson
Book Design: Mike Donnellan

Photo Credits: Cover (lower left), p. 15 © Weatherstock; p. 4 (left and bottom) © CORBIS; pp. 4 (second to left), 11 © Images Club Graphics, Inc.; p. 4 (second from right) © Jose Luis Pelaez, Inc./CORBIS; p. 4 (right) © Royalty Free/CORBIS; p. 8 © William Manning/CORBIS.

Library of Congress Cataloging-in-Publication Data

Estigarribia, Diana.
Learning about weather with graphic organizers / Diana Estigarribia.— 1st ed.
      v. cm. — (Graphic organizers in science)
Includes bibliographical references and index.
Contents: What is weather? — Temperature and sunshine — Air and wind — Clouds — Rain and storms — Extreme weather — Seasons — Climates — Weather forecasts.
ISBN 1-4042-2803-9 (lib. bdg.)
ISBN 1-4042-5036-0 (paperback)

1. Weather—Study and teaching (Elementary)—Graphic methods—Juvenile literature. [1. Weather.] I. Title. II. Series.
QC981.5 .E88 2005
372.35—dc22

2003018285

Manufactured in the United States of America

Contents

Tree Chart: Weather

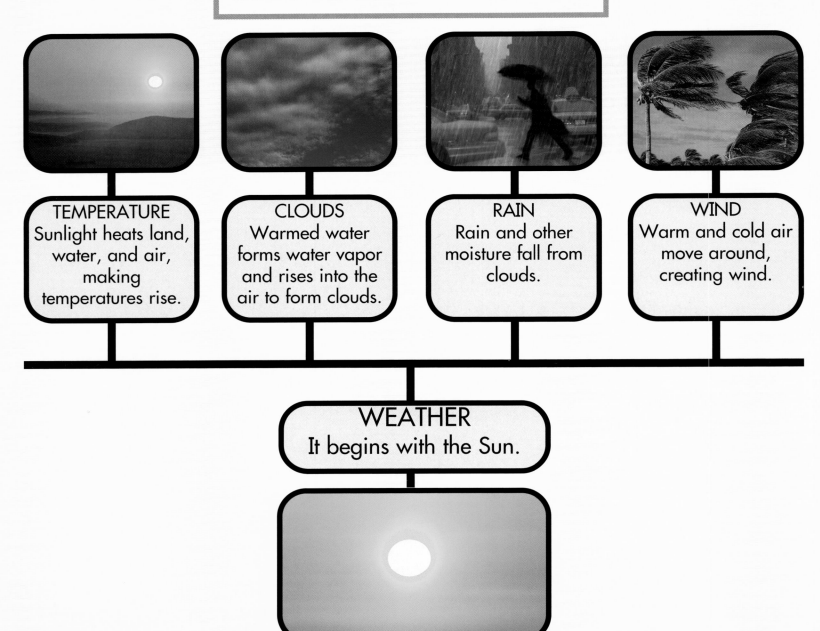

TEMPERATURE
Sunlight heats land, water, and air, making temperatures rise.

CLOUDS
Warmed water forms water vapor and rises into the air to form clouds.

RAIN
Rain and other moisture fall from clouds.

WIND
Warm and cold air move around, creating wind.

WEATHER
It begins with the Sun.

What Is Weather?

Weather is all the natural conditions that happen in Earth's **atmosphere**. Weather includes **temperature**, clouds, rain and other moisture, and wind. The atmosphere is the air around Earth. It reaches more than 600 miles (966 km) from the ground into the sky. The atmosphere acts like a blanket around Earth, holding in heat from the Sun. Scientists divide the atmosphere into layers. The layer closest to Earth is called the **troposphere**. It is from 5 to 11 miles (8–18 km) thick. It contains most of the atmosphere's gases, such as oxygen and nitrogen. Ninety-nine percent of all weather happens within the troposphere.

Graphic organizers are charts and other written tools that help to put information in order. In this book graphic organizers are used to organize information about weather.

This graphic organizer is called a tree chart. The subject of the chart, shown in the "trunk," is weather. The "branches" on the chart show the elements that are part of weather. The chart explains that temperature, clouds, rain and other moisture, and wind all begin with the Sun. Without the heat of the Sun, there would be no weather.

Sunshine and Temperature

Temperature is one part of weather that is easy to measure. If you walk outside, you know whether the air is hot or cold. To get an exact measurement, people use a **thermometer**. It measures temperature in degrees Fahrenheit or degrees Celsius.

Temperatures differ all over Earth because the Sun heats Earth unevenly. For example, in places where it is day, temperatures rise as sunlight warms the air. In places where it is night, temperatures fall. The angle of sunlight also affects temperature. Sunlight hits Earth most directly around the **equator**, the area midway between the North Pole and the South Pole. This area is the warmest on Earth. Temperatures get colder north and south of the equator, because Earth curves away from the Sun and sunlight reaches those areas indirectly.

A line graph shows how something changes over time. This line graph shows the change in average monthly temperatures, in degrees Fahrenheit, of three cities during one year. To find the temperature of any city for any month, trace straight up from the month until you reach the dot on the line that goes with that city. Then trace sideways to find the temperature.

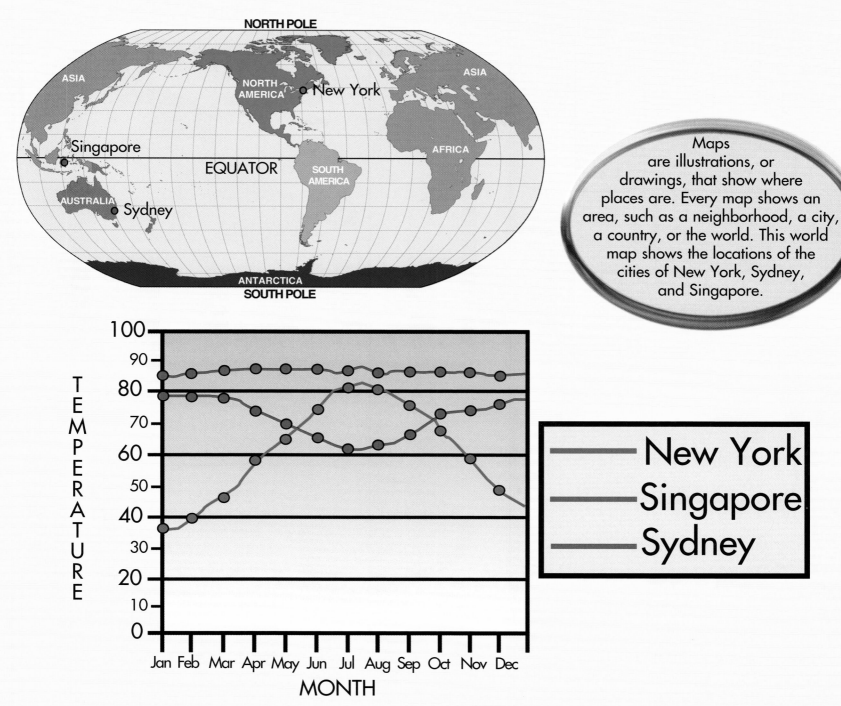

NORTH POLE

ASIA

NORTH AMERICA

New York

ASIA

Singapore

EQUATOR

AFRICA

SOUTH AMERICA

AUSTRALIA

Sydney

ANTARCTICA

SOUTH POLE

Maps are illustrations, or drawings, that show where places are. Every map shows an area, such as a neighborhood, a city, a country, or the world. This world map shows the locations of the cities of New York, Sydney, and Singapore.

TEMPERATURE

100
90
80
70
60
50
40
30
20
10
0

Jan Feb Mar Apr May Jun Jul Aug Sep Oct Nov Dec

MONTH

—— New York
—— Singapore
—— Sydney

Sequence Chart: Wind

Sunlight reaches Earth, heating land and water.

↓

Air above the land and water warms up.

↓

The warmed air expands, lightens, and rises into the troposphere, leaving an area of low air pressure beneath it.

↓

Colder air moves in to replace the rising warm air. The movement of the air is wind.

You cannot see wind, but you can see its effect on trees and sand. Winds can blow hard enough to bend and break trees and to move sand and dirt many feet (m) or even miles (km). You can also feel wind as it blows by you.

Air and Wind

The atmosphere works to balance uneven temperatures by moving air around. The movement of air is called wind. Wind causes weather to change. Wind is created by differences in air pressure, the weight of air pressing on the ground. When sunlight heats air, the air **molecules** move faster. They move apart, causing the air to **expand**, or take up more space. This makes the air lighter. The warm, light air rises and does not press as much on the ground. This is called low pressure. Cold air is heavier because its molecules are packed closer together. Cold air sinks and presses on the ground, creating an area of high pressure. It moves in to replace the rising warm air, creating wind. Wind speed is measured with a tool called an **anemometer**. Winds blow faster when an area of high pressure is close to an area of low pressure. Air pressure is measured with a barometer.

This graphic organizer is called a sequence chart. A sequence chart can help you to remember the order in which steps happen. Each arrow points to the next step. The steps of this sequence chart explain how air becomes wind.

Clouds

Clouds are part of weather conditions and can be signs of weather to come. Clouds form when air rises and cools in the troposphere. Air contains water vapor. The amount of water vapor in the air is measured as **humidity**. Humid air feels moist and sticky. Warm air can hold more water vapor than cold air can. As air cools, its molecules move closer together. The water vapor molecules in the air also move closer until they join and turn into water droplets. If water vapor joins at freezing temperatures, it forms ice crystals. The droplets or crystals are so light that they stay in the air as clouds. The three main types of clouds are **stratus**, **cumulus**, and **cirrus**. Stratus clouds are gray, layered clouds. Cumulus clouds are puffy and white with flat bottoms. Cirrus clouds are thin, feathery clouds. They form from ice crystals.

This is a chart about clouds. Charts are used to organize all kinds of information to make a topic easier to study. The topic subjects are listed in the far left column. More information about each subject is listed in the row to its right. The type of information that can be learned about the subjects is listed at the top of each column.

Chart: Clouds

Name	Height	Formation	Appearance	Weather	Example
Stratus	0–6,500 feet (0–1,981 m)	Stratus clouds form when a large area of air, called an air mass, is lifted by a colder air mass or by moving upward over hills.	Gray layers that cover the sky like a large blanket.	Overcast skies, may rain or snow lightly for a long time. Stratus clouds that form at ground level are called fog.	
Cumulus	2,000–10,000 feet (610–3,048 m)	Cumulus clouds form on sunny days from small areas of rising warm air. If the air is rising quickly, the clouds will be bigger.	Puffy and white with flat bottoms, like white cotton candy or ice cream.	Sunny skies, possible short rain showers. However, if cumulus clouds grow large, they may make heavy rain or snow.	
Cirrus	Above 16,500 feet (5,029 m)	Cirrus clouds form when water vapor joins high in the troposphere. At this height, the clouds are made of ice crystals.	Thin and feathery. Some cirrus clouds are said to look like horses' tails.	Large amounts of cirrus clouds may appear before stormy weather.	

KWL Chart: Stormy Weather

What I Know	What I Want to Know	What I Have Learned
• Rain is water.	• How does rain get into the sky?	• Rain forms when water vapor in the air turns back into liquid. At first the droplets of liquid water form a cloud. As the droplets join and become bigger droplets, they at last fall from the sky as rain.
• Snow is frozen water.	• Why are snow and rain different?	• Snow forms when the water vapor in the air freezes into ice crystals. The crystals grow bigger until they fall as snow.
• Lightning is bright.	• What makes lightning?	• Lightning is created by the buildup of electrical charges in a cumulonimbus cloud. Air moves up and down in the cloud, making water droplets and dust bump into each other, building up charges. Eventually the charges spark as lightning.
• Thunder is loud.	• Why do lightning and thunder always happen together?	• Thunder is the sound made by lightning heating the air superfast. Lightning heats the air to 54,000°F (30,000°C).

Stormy Weather

If water droplets or ice crystals in clouds continue to join, they can grow large enough to fall to the ground, creating wet weather. Moisture that falls from clouds is called **precipitation**. Precipitation falls as rain, snow, sleet, or hail, depending on temperatures in and around the clouds. For example, ice crystals that stay frozen fall as snow. However, if temperatures below the cloud are warm, the snow melts as it falls. It reaches the ground as rain. A storm is heavy precipitation with fast winds.

Thunderstorms are strong storms. Thunderstorm clouds, called **cumulonimbus** clouds, build from cumulus clouds on humid days when warm air rises quickly. The clouds build to the top of the troposphere. Then air and water in the clouds sink downward. The up-and-down movement of air and water in the clouds makes rain and electrical charges that create lightning and thunder.

This is a KWL chart. A KWL chart helps you to find out what you already know, what you want to know, and what you can learn from studying a subject. The third column, What I Have Learned, gets filled in as you study and learn the answers to your questions.

Extreme Weather

Thunderstorms can make even more **extreme** weather. When many thunderstorms gather over oceans where water temperatures are at least 80°F (27°C), they may form a storm called a hurricane. Earth's spinning movement causes the thunderstorms to move into a thick circle of storms that can be hundreds of miles (km) wide. If the storm winds reach a speed of 74 miles per hour (120 km/h), the circle of storms is called a hurricane.

About 1 in 1,000 thunderstorms on land will form a tornado. A tornado begins when the winds near the top of a storm blow faster and in a different direction than the winds below. This makes the thunderstorm turn. Air inside the storm cloud spins into a column of air called a funnel. The funnel spins downward. If the funnel touches the ground it is called a tornado.

This graphic organizer is called a Venn diagram. Venn diagrams organize the features of different things to show how they are different and what they have in common. The features the things have in common go in the middle area, where the diagram circles overlap. This Venn diagram compares the features of a hurricane and a tornado.

Hurricane winds can reach a speed of 180 miles per hour (290 km/h).

Tornados can move 100 feet per second (30.5 m/s). Winds in the funnel can spin at 250 miles per hour (402 km/h).

Venn Diagram

Hurricane

Tornado

- Forms over water

- Is hundreds of miles (km) wide

- Occurs in summer and fall

- Causes high waves

- Forms from thunderstorms

- Has high winds

- Spins

- Can cause much harm

- Forms over land

- Is usually less than 1 mile (1.6 km) wide

- Has a thin funnel that can suck up and move things such as cars and animals

- Occurs at any time of year

Cycle: The Four Seasons

SUMMER

Temperatures are at their highest. Grass and other plants may dry up and turn yellow. In many places, precipitation falls as rain and sometimes as hail. Thunderstorms are common. Hurricanes may form over the ocean.

FALL

Days get shorter and nights get longer. Temperatures drop. Frost may form in the morning. Precipitation falls as rain or snow. Leaves change color and fall off trees. Animals such as squirrels store food for winter. Some animals begin to grow thick fur.

SPRING

Temperatures grow warm. Snow melts. Plants show new growth. Flowers blossom. Precipitation falls as rain in many places. Days get longer and nights get shorter. Many animals give birth to their young.

WINTER

Temperatures are at their lowest. Days are short and nights are long. Precipitation may fall as snow and sleet. Lakes and rivers freeze. Some animals stay in their dens through winter.

Seasons

Weather changes regularly in seasons on Earth. Some places on Earth have two seasons and some have four. A place's location on Earth is measured in degrees **latitude**. The equator is at 0 degrees latitude. The North Pole is at 90 degrees north. The South Pole is at 90 degrees south. Places between 23.5 degrees north and 23.5 degrees south have two seasons, wet and dry. This area is called the tropics. The United States is located between 25 and 50 degrees north latitude. It has four seasons. Winter weather is cool and rainy in the southern United States and cold and snowy in the north. Temperatures grow warm in spring, and most places get rain. Summers are hot in the south and warm in the north. Many places get rain and thunderstorms. In fall, temperatures cool off as days grow shorter. The leaves on many trees change color and fall off as winter comes again.

This organizer is called a cycle. A cycle shows a series of events that has no beginning and no end, but that always occurs again and again in the same order. This cycle graph shows the four seasons. The United States is one place on Earth that has four seasons.

Climates

The pattern of weather conditions in an area over a long period of time is called its climate. Yearly average temperature and precipitation create climate type. Tropical climates are found near the equator. They are always warm. More than 100 inches (254 cm) of rain may fall every year. Farther north and south of the equator are temperate and dry climates. Warm temperate places have hot summers and mild, rainy winters. Cool temperate places have warm summers and cold winters with snow. Arid, or dry, climates are the driest. They include areas where just enough rain falls for grass to grow, and deserts, where few plants grow. Mountainous areas have highland climates. They are cold high on the peaks and warmer toward the mountain bases. Polar climates are the coldest. They have long, dark winters and cool summers. They get little or no precipitation.

This organizer is called a compare/contrast chart. A compare/contrast chart can help you to compare the features of related subjects. In this chart, world climates are compared for the features in the left column, which are temperature, precipitation, and usual weather.

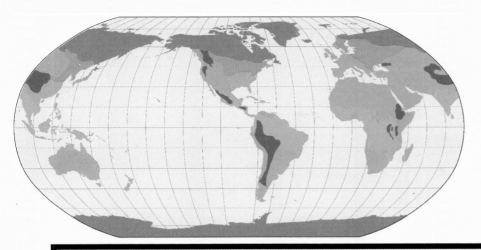

Legend:
- Tropical
- Dry
- Warm Temperate
- Cool Temperate
- Highland
- Polar

Compare/Contrast Chart: World Climates

	Tropical	Dry	Warm Temperate	Cool Temperate	Highland	Polar
Temperature	Above 64°F (18°C) year-round.	Highs of 70°F to 120°F (21–49°C), lows below freezing.	Highs in the 90s°F (30s°C), lows above 27°F (-3°C).	Highs in the 90s°F (30s°C), lows below 27°F (-3°C).	Wide range. As height goes up, Temperatures go down. Highlands may be warm at the base and freezing at the top.	Below 50°F (10°C) in the north, always below freezing in the south.
Yearly Precipitation	More than 59 inches (150 cm), and more that 100 inches (254 cm) in rain forests.	Less than ½ inch (1.3 cm) to 11 inches (28 cm).	16 to 68 inches (41–173 cm).	Up to 40 inches (102 cm). Some places get little precipitation.	Depends on the climate of the area around the highland.	Very little, mostly snow.
Usual Weather	Either very heavy rain year-round, or a lot of rain with a few dry summer months.	Little or no rain. Hot during the day and cold at night. Hot summers, cool winters.	In the east, humid, warm summers. In the west, dry, warm to hot summers. Cool summers on coasts. Mild winters.	Warm to cool summers and cold, windy winters with snow.	Much colder at night than during the day. Snow may fall on mountain peaks even in the summer. Cool summers, freezing winters.	Cool to freezing summers, freezing cold winters.

19

Timeline: A History of Weather-Measuring Tools

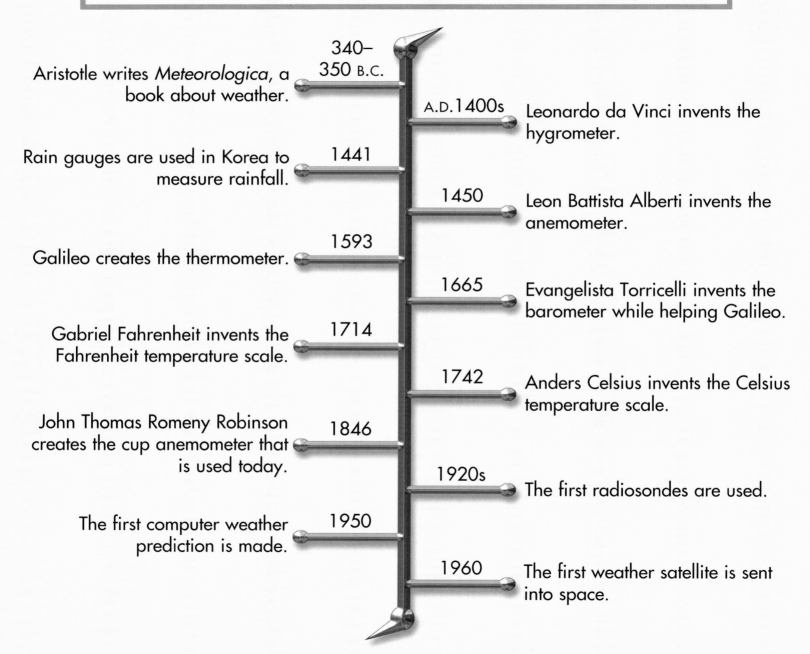

Aristotle writes *Meteorologica*, a book about weather. — 340–350 B.C.

A.D. 1400s — Leonardo da Vinci invents the hygrometer.

Rain gauges are used in Korea to measure rainfall. — 1441

1450 — Leon Battista Alberti invents the anemometer.

Galileo creates the thermometer. — 1593

1665 — Evangelista Torricelli invents the barometer while helping Galileo.

Gabriel Fahrenheit invents the Fahrenheit temperature scale. — 1714

1742 — Anders Celsius invents the Celsius temperature scale.

John Thomas Romeny Robinson creates the cup anemometer that is used today. — 1846

1920s — The first radiosondes are used.

The first computer weather prediction is made. — 1950

1960 — The first weather satellite is sent into space.

Weather Forecasts

The study of weather conditions is called meteorology. Meteorologists are scientists who measure weather. They study weather conditions so that they can forecast the weather for the next day or the rest of the week. Weather is forecast by taking readings of temperature, air pressure, humidity, wind direction and speed, and by checking **visibility**, type of clouds, and precipitation. Tools used to gather readings include the thermometer for temperature, the barometer for pressure, the **hygrometer** for humidity, the weather vane for wind direction, and the anemometer for wind speed. Readings are collected by ships, airplanes, **radar**, **satellites**, and **radiosondes**. A radiosonde is a small package of weather-measuring tools. It is carried into the sky by a special balloon. Throughout the world about 1,000 radiosondes are let loose twice per day to take weather readings.

This graphic organizer is called a timeline. Timelines list a series of events in the order, by year, in which they happened. Making a timeline can help you to remember when something happened and the order in which several events happened.

Future Weather

Future weather will depend on natural forces and human actions that affect heat and the atmosphere. The gases in the atmosphere trap sunlight and help to warm Earth. This is called the **greenhouse effect**. It is necessary for life on Earth. Without it, Earth's average temperature would drop from 58°F (14°C) to about −2°F (−19°C). However, too many greenhouse gases can cause Earth's average temperature to rise too much. Over the past 100 years, it has risen about 1°F (.56°C). This rise is called **global warming**. Human actions have caused the global warming of the past 50 years. Human use of fuels has created more greenhouse gases. Most scientists believe that global warming will cause weather patterns to change. Extreme weather may happen more often. Sea levels may rise. Today scientists and governments are working to find ways to stop global warming.

Glossary

anemometer (a-neh-MAH-meh-tur) A tool used to measure wind speed.

atmosphere (AT-muh-sfeer) The layers of air around Earth.

cirrus (SER-us) A type of cloud that is feathery and thin.

cumulonimbus (kyoo-myuh-loh-NIM-bus) Clouds that bring thunderstorms.

cumulus (KYOO-myuh-lus) Puffy, white clouds with flat bottoms.

equator (ih-KWAY-tur) An imaginary line around Earth that separates it into two parts, northern and southern.

expand (ek-SPAND) Spread out, or grow larger.

extreme (ek-STREEM) Much better or worse than average.

global warming (GLOH-bul WARM-ing) A gradual rise in how hot Earth is. It is caused by gases that are created when people burn fuels, such as gasoline.

graphic organizers (GRA-fik OR-guh-ny-zerz) Charts, graphs, and pictures that sort facts and ideas and make them clear.

greenhouse effect (GREEN-hows eh-FEKT) Heat trapped by the gases in the air around Earth.

humidity (hyoo-MIH-dih-tee) The amount of moisture in the air.

hygrometer (hy-GRAH-meh-ter) A tool used to measure the amount of moisture in the air.

latitude (LA-tih-tood) The distance north or south of the equator, measured by degrees.

molecules (MAH-lih-kyoolz) The smallest bits of matter.

precipitation (preh-sih-pih-TAY-shun) Any moisture that falls from the sky, such as rain and snow.

radar (RAY-dar) A tool that uses radio waves to take weather readings.

radiosondes (RAY-dee-oh-sondz) Weather balloons.

satellites (SA-til-yts) Machines in space that circle Earth and that are used to track weather.

stratus (STRA-tus) Large, flat, gray clouds.

temperature (TEM-pruh-chur) The amount of heat in an object or the air.

thermometer (thur-MAH-meh-tur) A tool used to measure how hot or cold something is.

troposphere (TROH-puh-sfeer) The layer of air closest to Earth in which weather happens.

visibility (vih-zeh-BIH-leh-tee) The amount of clearness of the air.

Index

Web Sites

Due to the changing nature of Internet links, PowerKids Press has developed an online list of Web sites related to the subject of this book. This site is updated regularly. Please use this link to access the list:
www.powerkidslinks.com/gosci/weathergo/